CELEBRATING DAY OF THE DEAD

BY THEODORE JONES

Gareth Stevens
PUBLISHING

Please visit our website, www.garethstevens.com. For a free color catalog of all our high-quality books, call toll free 1-800-542-2595 or fax 1-877-542-2596.

Library of Congress Cataloging-in-Publication Data

Jones, Theodore (Theodore Francis), 1978- author.
 Celebrating Day of the Dead / Theodore Jones.
     pages cm. — (The history of our holidays)
 Includes bibliographical references and index.
 Summary: El Día de los Muertos is celebrated in Mexico with food and festivities to celebrate life and to honor and remember deceased loved ones.
 ISBN 978-1-4824-3886-4 (pbk.)
 ISBN 978-1-4824-3887-1 (6 pack)
 ISBN 978-1-4824-3888-8 (library binding)
 1. All Souls' Day—Mexico—Juvenile literature. 2. Mexico—Social life and customs—Juvenile literature. I. Title.
 GT4995.A4J66 2016
 394.266—dc23

                                    2015018173

Published in 2016 by
Gareth Stevens Publishing
111 East 14th Street, Suite 349
New York, NY 10003

Copyright © 2016 Gareth Stevens Publishing

Designer: Sarah Liddell
Editor: Therese Shea

Photo credits: Cover, p. 1 cvalle/Shutterstock.com; p. 5 tipograffias/Shutterstock.com; p. 7 sunsinger/Shutterstock.com; p. 9 DEA/G. DAGLI ORTI/Contributor/De Agostini/ Getty Images; p. 11 PHAS/Contributor/Universal Images Group/Getty Images; p. 13 Jose Gil/Shutterstock.com; p. 15 AGCuesta/Shutterstock.com; p. 17 Nathalie Speliers Ufermann/Shutterstock.com; p. 18 Chad Zuber/Shutterstock.com; p. 19 Patricia Aranda/Contributor/Moment Mobile/Getty Images; p. 21 (left) Kobby Dagan/Shutterstock.com; p. 21 (right) Hugo Brizard/Shutterstock.com.

Printed in the United States of America

CPSIA compliance information: Batch #CW16GS: For further information contact Gareth Stevens, New York, New York at 1-800-542-2595.

CONTENTS

A Day for the Dead 4

Ancient Holiday 8

Traditions 12

Celebrating Life 20

Glossary 22

For More Information 23

Index 24

Boldface words appear in the glossary.

A Day for the Dead

Have you ever heard of the Day of the Dead? It might sound scary, but it's not. It's a holiday to honor and **celebrate** loved ones who have died. It's not a sad holiday, though. There are many interesting, fun **traditions**!

In Spanish, the Day of the Dead is called Día de los Muertos (DEE-ah DEH LOHS MUEHR-tohs). The holiday is mostly celebrated in Mexico and other parts of **Latin America**. Many people celebrate it in the United States, too.

Ancient Holiday

The Aztecs were people who once lived in what's now Mexico. Each summer, they had a month-long celebration to honor a goddess called "Lady of the Dead." They made food for the dead. They also made clay figures of them.

9

When the Spanish came to Mexico in the 1500s, the holiday was moved from summer to fall. Instead of a month, it was 1 or 2 days. Many people in Mexico now celebrate the Day of the Dead on November 1 and 2.

Traditions

In Mexico, people visit the **graves** of their loved ones on the first day of the holiday. They place flowers and candles on them. They may have a **picnic** near the graves, too. Often, the whole community is there!

Special food is part of the day. *Pan de muerto* is bread shaped like a person or like bones. There's a small plastic toy hidden in it! Many people think it's good luck to bite the toy.

People also give each other gifts to celebrate the Day of the Dead. They often have something to do with death, such as sugar **skulls**. People eat these. It's a way to show they're not afraid of death.

Some people celebrate the Day of the Dead at home. They build **altars** and place yellow and orange flowers on them. They put photos of loved ones on the altar. They might place favorite foods and drinks on it, too.

Celebrating Life

The Day of the Dead may seem to focus on dead loved ones. However, it has more to do with honoring life. That's why you may see people dressed as happy, dancing **skeletons** on this day. Celebrate Día de Los Muertos!

GLOSSARY

altar: a raised place or table on which gifts are offered in some religions and traditions

celebrate: to honor with special activities

grave: a burial place

Latin America: the land south of the United States

picnic: a meal eaten outdoors away from home

skeleton: the set of bones that supports a body

skull: the bones of the head

tradition: a long-practiced custom or way of life

FOR MORE INFORMATION

BOOKS

Axelrod-Contrada, Joan. *Halloween and Day of the Dead Traditions Around the World*. Mankato, MN: Child's World, 2013.

Gleason, Carrie. *Day of the Dead*. New York, NY: Crabtree Publishing, 2009.

Murray, Julie. *Day of the Dead*. Edina, MN: ABDO Publishing Company, 2014.

WEBSITES

Dia de los Muertos
education.nationalgeographic.com/education/media/dia-de-los-muertos/
Check out amazing pictures of this celebration.

Dia de los Muertos
www.dayofthedeadsf.org/history.html
Find out more about this special celebration for the dead.

Publisher's note to educators and parents: Our editors have carefully reviewed these websites to ensure that they are suitable for students. Many websites change frequently, however, and we cannot guarantee that a site's future contents will continue to meet our high standards of quality and educational value. Be advised that students should be closely supervised whenever they access the Internet.

INDEX

altars 18

Aztecs 8

candles 12

Día de los Muertos 6, 20

flowers 12, 18

food 8, 14, 18

gifts 16

graves 12

Lady of the Dead 8

Latin America 6

loved ones 4, 12, 18, 20

Mexico 6, 8, 10, 12

pan de muerto 14

photos 18

picnic 12

skeletons 20

Spanish 10

sugar skulls 16

traditions 4